LINE DANCING

ANGELIQUE FERNANDEZ
& KAREN FARRINGTON

GREENWICH EDITIONS

This edition published 1997 by the
Promotional Reprint Company Ltd,
Kiln House, 210 New Kings Road, London SW6 4NZ

Produced for Greenwich Editions
Bibliophile House,
10, Blenheim Court, Brewery Road
London, N7 9NT

ISBN 0 86288 146 3

Printed and bound in China

CONTENTS

The Cast
The dancers:

Angelique Fenandez
Harley Marshall
Hughie Thom
Ian Lennie
Joanne White

INTRODUCTION

IN THE 1940s it was the jitterbug. In the Fifties it was the twist. The Nineties now has a new dance craze to call its own. Line Dancing is the toe- tapping, hand-clapping, high-stepping sensation that has swept the world

Although its roots are in the country and western scene, line dancers come from all walks of life and span every musical peccadillo. Some are opera buffs, others like heavy metal. Put them together for classic line dances like the Watermelon Crawl, Bad Dog Boogie or an Armadillo and they are rhythmic twins. Line Dancing has young, old, far, slender, city slicker and city refuse collector moving as one. That's a major part of its appeal.

How, why and from where did this amazing phenomenon emerge to sweep the global music scene? Chances are that it was created by the early immigrant prospectors in the US and is an amalgamation of European cultures, including Irish jigs and Scottish reels. But its cult status seems to have started in America in the late Seventies — possibly emanating from Nashville, possibly from a popular dance exhibition staged by Arizona hotels.

Since then, the Line Dance phenomenon has breathed new life into the Country scene worldwide. Sales of Western-style boots, belts, gypsy blouses, tiered skirts, flared minis and Stetsons are booming. There are videos, CDs and magazines. Fitness instructors, bowing to demand, are teaching toe spreads, scuffs and shuffles.

Yet Line Dancing is only what YOU want to make of it... The gear is as modest or as expensive as you want it to be. Jeans, cowboy boots and Stetson hats are the norm for men, while women choose either flowing tiered skirts and gypsy blouses or short, flared skirts and T-shirts.

And the good news about the dances themselves is that you don't need a partner! Line dancers go it alone and get their kicks in executing synchronised steps at speed. There are dances for couples but most of the new clubs springing up cater only for line dancers.

Line Dancing is great exercise — without inflicting 'the burn'. It takes your mind away from daily strife and, best of all, it's fun.

Quite simply, dancers line up in straight rows and move in unison, usually to the sounds of 'New Country' — a cross between rock and country

music, with a bit of new wave thrown in for good measure. At the head of the dancers is an instructor who is there to remind both old hands and newcomers of the dances and steps.

The number of routines available to dancers is mushrooming. Line Dancing may be the babe-in-arms of the dance world yet there are already more than 1,000 different dances in existence and more are being created by the day. Among the more exotically titled dances found in America are the Salty Dog Rag, California Tanglefoot, Anthracite Rose Stroll, Ukiah 20 Step Toot Toot and the Slam Dunk. In Britain the bizarrely called dances include Scootch, Cajun Mambo Walk, Boot Scootin's Boogie and Thunderfoot.

At Line Dancing festivals, the steps of new routines are swapped and quickly spread through the clubs.

This book is especially for beginners. It has got everything you need to know about what to wear, how to wear it, line-dancing 'do's' and 'don'ts', the steps and, of course, a generous wedge of dances to get you started. So when you finally swop the security of your living room for the Line Dancing club you will be able to shuffle, slide and strut with the best of the rest.

MEET ANGELIQUE

TO HELP YOU with your first, faltering steps into the world of line-dancing we bring you Angelique Fernandez, your own personal instructor. Angelique is a New Yorker by birth who lives in London and runs a successful Line Dancing company called Sunset Stampede. Angelique will give you the facts about Line Dancing as well as her personal philosophy which makes her classes the most sought after around.

Her mother was from the Dominican Republic, her father was of Cuban stock. But Angelique's ancestors were from across the globe and she has French, Danish, Corsican and Puerto Rican blood coursing through her veins. From this rich heritage she draws her love of dance.

Yet her very first job was about as remote from the dance floor as it is possible to get. After leaving school Angelique joined the peace corps, the American equivalent of Britain's Voluntary Service Overseas. That took her to North Yemen in one of the first western missions to the devout Islamic country.

Globe-trotting Angelique first came across Line Dancing when she later spent two and a half years working with the United States Organisation supporting overseas troops. She was in Seoul, South Korea, when she stumbled on the phenomena. Its advantages were immediately obvious.

'There were 11 guys to every female on a good day. Line Dancing was an ideal social survival kit for the single person,' she explained. The seeds of an obsession were sown.

In 1993 she went for a skiing trip to Nevada where she broke her wrist. She found herself in a corner of America where Line Dancing is as much a part of the culture as hamburgers and Hershey bars. The injury transformed a six- week snow boarding holiday into a seven-month line dance fest and Angelique left ready to spread the gospel of Line Dancing. She came to Europe and taught in London and Ireland.

For a while she struggle to uncover a lively country scene in England. Then Line Dancing took off big-time. Angelique was hired to start the Outlaws and Sinners Line Dancing club in 1994, at Ashton's in Cricklewood, North West London. Every week she still teaches hundreds of people there.

So phenomenal was the response to Line Dancing that Angelique formed Sunset Stampede, a company especially concerned with the new craze employing more instructors to carry the word into the home counties. In March 1995 Sunset Stampede released its first instructional video to help all those who couldn't reach one of her gigs. After the dance party video was released in April 1995 it shot to number 12 in the national sales charts.

At Angelique's hugely popular dances you are likely to find the Silent Cowboys, an awesome looking crowd from the local bikers' club who have become addicted to Line Dancing. Hughie Thom, a maintenance engineer at Heathrow airport, caught the Line Dancing bug on holiday in the States three years ago. When he returned he taught his mates the basics and they, too, became smitten.

There's one liberating cornerstone to Angelique's teaching which all her students must bear in mind.

'There are no mistakes in Line Dancing. There is only improvisation,' says Angelique. 'That makes every dancer a champion because there are no failures, no criticisms and no place for grouchy perfectionists.'

HISTORY OF LINE DANCING

LINE DANCING SEEMED like the phenomenon that came from nowhere. In fact, it came from just about everywhere.

With a little careful scrutiny plenty of elements of previous popular dance forms can be identified in Line Dancing. And that's not surprising, given that every dance form borrows a little from the one before. Line Dancing — being the latest to emerge — has a colourful history upon which to draw.

Trace the roots of Line Dancing and you must delve back thousands of years. Dancing in a line was one of the earliest forms of entertainment. There's even a theory that ancient man lined up for some ritual dance steps with his fellows, the roaring fire throwing eerie shadows on to the wall of their caves. The aim of their dance was to ward off evil spirits.

Later, in ancient Greece, dancing in a line was a revered pastime, and in their national dance it still thrives today. Scottish and Irish dancing were often singular experiences although not necessarily in a line. In Europe the emphasis was more on polkas, the minuet or clog dancing.

The Scots might have continued their reels in isolation and the Germans would have probably clogged on alone without the mighty waves of emigrants to America from Europe during the 1800s. There a clutch of cultures came together and slowly melded into one.

Romantically-minded folk like to believe that 'Forty-Niner' miners of the Californian gold rush whiled away their long evenings by line dancing in front of the camp fire. There are those who firmly declare that cowboys in the wild west were avid line dancers. Jesse James and the Younger boys may have been closet line dancers but there's absolutely no evidence that either them or any other gunslingers or ranchers were smitten with the tush push.

Bear in mind, too, that during the 19th century dancing alone or with a partner was regarded as unwholesome. In Colorado Territory during the last century there were 300 unfortunate dance masters hanged or tarred and feathered because of their 'inappropriate behaviour'.

It was out of German clog dancing, Irish country dancing and the entertainment made by the Afro American slaves that tap dancing emerged. The emphasis like Line Dancing was on foot and leg movements. From jazz dancing we get Line Dancing's jazz box.

At about the same time the Charleston swept America and this, too, has been included in the range of Line Dancing steps. Thirty years on the cha cha arrived from Cuba, an exotic notion that likewise has found a place in line dance.

Take a quick look too at barn and square dancing to find that bits of both folk dance forms have been imported into the line. Square dances had callers while line dances have instructors.

There are those who claim Line Dancing was born in Nashville while other believe it was spawned during a music festival hosted in a string of Arizona hotels. Perhaps the father of modern line dancing is Jim Ferrazzano who choreographed such classics as Tush Push, Waltz Across Texas and of course, Flying 8s.

His personal experience gives us the best insight into the recent history of line dancing. He learned his first line dance at a honky tonk when he was nine years old. At the time and throughout the sixties Line Dancing was known as 'outlaw dancing' performed to outlaw music. The roguish nature of the dancers had nothing to do with its title, however. It was because the dance was on the fringe, an underground movement kept well away from the mainstream. Fellow outlaws included Waylon Jennings and Willie Nelson.

Excited by the possibilities revealed in early line dancing, Ferrazzano choreographed tush push in 1980 in Charleston, South Carolina. He received hate mail for his trouble, from those who were concerned that line dancing threatened the established country and western scene. A split between die-hard country and western fans and line dancers exists in some quarters to this very day.

One important emissary for Line Dancing was the US servicemen and women who helped to export the craze overseas. In tandem with this blossoming craze was a growing awareness of dance in general and its possibilities, which was constantly reinforced popular culture.

American Graffiti, in 1973, reminded people about the potential of the stroll. John Travolta in *Saturday Night Fever,* released in 1978, enlivened an otherwise dreary urban tragedy with some exciting dance routines. In the same year the ever-popular, ebullient motion picture *Grease* was unleashed onto cinema audiences. The pupils of Rydell High hand-jiving in lines had a riveting effect. A decade later the film *Hairspray* revived a sixties step known as the madison.

Proof that line dancing was achieving cult status began came in the compelling road movie *Thelma and Louise*. The 1991 film showed how a country and western bar in Arkansas was transformed when clubbers began toeing the line to some rocking new country sounds.

The disco dance-mania of the 1970s had flagged – yet still people wanted to dance. They were ready to welcome line dancing, bred out of so many different dances, with open arms.

In Australia line dancing also found a natural home. There they call it boot-scootin' and it is as likely to take place in a massive pub car park in the outback as it will in the dance halls of Sydney or Canberra.

Line dancing has happily remained free of red tape. There are no exams or grades to strive for and the only imposed discipline is self-discipline. While private companies have concocted certificates for line dancing instructors there are no regulations issued by a relevant national body which says they are a must. Should you go to a line dance class and loathe it then you will vote with your feet and find another, regardless of what pieces of paper are brandished in your face.

And there was another key reason which has made line dancing ideal for the modern era. Single women have felt increasingly vulnerable when they danced at close quarters with strangers. With line dancing they can still meet new people between numbers without risking a mauling. Don't forget that plenty of enthusiastic dancers have been sidelined because they have partners who would not be seen dead on the dance floor.

Line dancing empowers everyone to get on the floor, be they married, single, old, young, male or female. At last the age of equality has a worthy dance partner.

HISTORY OF NEW COUNTRY

LIKE EVERY DANCE form, music is the beating heart of the line. But if you're expecting C&W (Country and Western) music of the Jim Reeves or Patsy Kline ilk, then think again. There's no droning or 'doe si doe' as far as today's line dancing is concerned.

'A lot of people in Britain still believe that country music is the kind which says: "I'm alone in my saddle and my dog's just died". It's not like that any more,' says Angelique. She views the term C&W as something like a kiss of death. When it comes to describing the best music for line dancing she uses the more telling description of American New Country.

There's no doubt that C&W has exerted its influence over the music favoured by line dancers. And, after all, its tradition is long and broad, its numerous forms as contrasting as Beethoven and The Beatles. True, it was once possible to make certain assumptions about the music and the people associated with C&W. Years ago the music was mainly made by stringed instruments — brass sections were unknown — while the lyrics were simple. The sound has usually appealed to a particular group of people with certain attitudes and a set way of life.

When country music first made an impact the audience comprised those born and raised in rural settings in America's south or southwest. Generally speaking, this meant working-class white people, who were very patriotic, politically and religiously conservative, and who above all, defended the old ideals.

The sound began to spread when families migrated from those settings to the great northern cities, taking their musical tastes with them. As these musical preferences blended with other types of music, the forms changed and multiplied. And with the change in lifestyle came a marked difference in the song content. When once a song about divorce would have seemed blasphemous to those upright folk of the southern states, people in the industrial centres of the north could identify strongly with it.

Throughout the century the audience has mushroomed. It crosses race, creed and class. No longer can C&W be accused of being monotonous, humdrum or dreary, for if one Country song fits that description, the next dozen do not. Its appeal has never been so wide and its definitions so blurred. Had C&W retained its original southern states' format, it probably would never have gathered the same international momentum. But as time went by it incorporated more styles, adopted new aspects and continued to reinvent itself before arriving at American New Country.

First there was hillbilly music, a term which encompassed the entire country sound. Eventually, though, the word hillbilly became an insult. Country music pioneer Ernest Tubb made efforts to change the name to 'country and western' and the term was finally adopted by the 1950s. The loss of the hillbilly did not go unmourned. In the 1960s came a new song, titled: *Don't Call Us Hillbillies; We're Mountain Williams Now.*

Abroad, cinema goers believed C&W to be the songs sung by cowboys in the saddle in the films of the 1930s and 1940s. It was a different and altogether more complex story in the US.

There was the 'Bakersfield Sound', the music played by a group of musicians who lived in and around Bakersfield, California, in the late 1950s and early 1960s. Among its stars were Buck Owens, Merle Haggard, and Wynn Stewart.

Bluegrass music — the 'high, lonesome sound' — places emphasis on rhythm, coupled with instrumental skill. It takes its name from Bill Monroe's band, the Bluegrass Boys who hailed from Kentucky, the 'Bluegrass State'. Bluegrass is akin to jazz but remains a country genre thanks to the exclusive use of stringed instruments and because the lyrical content of bluegrass is similar to that of classic country music.

Another element to C&W was Cajun music, spawned among the exiled Canadian French who settled in Louisiana. Its hallmark was the language — the local *patois,* a form of French. Also, many Cajun bands include an accordion player *and* a fiddler, and most songs are played in a simple three-quarter waltz time.

From Spain comes Conjunto. The term, which means 'band' in Spanish, refers to a style of music popular along the border between Mexico and the United States.

Country blues has its place in the heritage of C&W, the music made by white singers who favour a black style, as has gospel music and honky tonk. The term 'honky tonk' was first used in a song title in 1937, but it didn't become widespread until the 1940s. Originally, a honky tonk was a squalid bar frequently by hard-drinking, loud-living wasters. Musicians there introduced amplification so their music could be heard over the hubbub.

The 'Nashville Sound' is easily distinguishable. A group of musicians working in Nashville in the late 1950s and early 1960s were taken up by the powerful record companies and given a uniform sound: an appreciative audience lapped it up. The sophistication of Nashville performers like Jim Reeves won it the accolade of 'countrypolitan'.

In opposition came the Outlaws who objected to being creatively controlled by the record company giants. They worked on their own compositions outside the strictures of Nashville. Among the Outlaws were Waylon Jennings, Willie Nelson, Billy Joe Shaver and Kris Kristofferson. The term 'outlaw' is now outdated but it was revived when RCA released an album of old tracks called *The Outlaws.* It became the first country album to be certified platinum by the Recording Industry Association of America. While Nashville was pumping out its brand of C&W, rockabilly — a mix of rock, rhythm & blues and country — was making headway elsewhere in America. It was the 1950s and the key musicians were Elvis Presley, Jerry Lee Lewis, Carl Perkins and Johnny Cash. Eventually the two strands came together at Nashville with outstanding results.

Given that southern rock, progressive country, western swing and Tex-Mex are all competing for their place in the C&W line up, it is apparent that new country has a proud birthright.

The two songs which have done most for line dancing internationally are *Achy Braky* and *Cotton Eyed Joe.* Sensationally breaking out of the country scene both records were chart-toppers in 1993 and each was cleverly packaged with a line dance of its own. Among the hot America New Country stars to look out for are Wynonna, Michelle Wright, Faith Hill, Shelby Lynne, Tricia Yearwood, Ricochet, Sammy Kershaw and LeAnn McBride.

The sound of New Country has travelled swiftly to Britain, thanks partly to the first country cable station and the first dedicated 24-hour station. This modern music has brought countless keen line dancers to the floor. But not without considerable fall out among some of the old-timers. Rosemary Claridge, who runs Claridge's Country Music Club, has watched with trepidation as a conflict grows. 'For years the music came first and the dancing came second. Now dancing is tending to over-ride the music. We go to a great deal of trouble sorting out bands. Long-time fans know the band and they know the value of that band. They come to listen.' Couples tempted to the dance floor for a waltz might find themselves in collision with a line dancer — and quickly discover that three is a crowd.

Angelique too has her doubts that line dancers can share the floor with couples. Yet she is convinced that American New Country heralds a great future for C&W. 'It's got to evolve to continue,' she says. The divisions have ultimately led to separate clubs for each genre . . .

NEW COUNTRY TIMELINE

1900	The word "hillbillie" first appears in print in the April 23 edition of the New York Journal.
1922	On June 30 "Uncle" Eck Robertson and Henry Gilliand record what is generally considered to be the first country music record. The place is New York and the record label is Victor. Both are fiddle tunes, "Sallie Goodin" and "The Arkansas Traveller."
1923	"Little Old Log Cabin in the Lane," recorded by Ralph Peer in Atlanta is considered to be country music's first hit record.
1924	"The Prisoner's Song," by Vernon Dalhart is the first country record ever to sell a million copies.
1925	On November 28 the "WSM Barn Dance," which later became "Grand Ole Opry," was first broadcast from WSM's Studio A in Nashville.
1930	Ken Maynard, starring in Song of the Saddle, is Hollywood's first singing cowboy.
1935	Patsy Montana records "I Want to Be a Cowboy's Sweetheart," the first country record by a female singer to sell a million copies.
1941	Pop star Bing Crosby breeches country and national boundaries when his songs "You Are My Sunshine" and "New San Antonio Rose," are hits, probably the first 'crossover' from country to occur. Electric guitars are first used on country music records.
1942	Elton Britt's "There's a Star-Spangled Banner Waving Somewhere," a song about a disabled boy who wants to help with the war effort, is country music's first gold record.
1953	Bill Haley's Saddle Pals release "Crazy, Man, Crazy" under the name Bill Haley and the Comets, the first country band to switch to rock and roll.
1954	The pedal steel guitar was first used on record, played by Bud Isaacs on Webb Pierce 's "Slowly."
1956	The first rock and roll sessions in Nashville are held in January. Elvis Presley records his first RCA release, "Heartbreak Hotel." Twenty days later (January 20), Buddy Holly cuts "Blue Days Black Nights," backed with "Love Me."
1961	On November 3 Fred Rose, Hank Williams, and Jimmie Rodgers are the first members of the Country Music Hall of Fame.
1966	Bob Dylan is the first of the new generation of rock singers to cut a major album in Nashville when he makes Blonde on Blonde .
1967	The first Country Music Association Awards show is held in October.
1969	Hee Haw, the country television show, makes its debut.
1970	Ringo Starr is the first Beatle to record in Nashville. Paul McCartney followed suit later.
1974	George Hamilton IV tours the Soviet Union, the first country performer to do so.
1976	Wanted: The Outlaws, an RCA album featuring Waylon Jennings and Willie Nelson is the first country music record to go platinum.
1980	The Tush Push is written by Jim Ferrazzano in South Carolina.
1993	Achy Braky and Cotton Eyed Joe enjoy international success and bring designated line dances to the fore.

WHAT TO WEAR

IT'S YOUR FIRST night at the local Line Dancing club and you want to make an impression when you step through the door. What's more, it's got to be the right impression. Don't worry, help is at hand. Angelique has a dress code which will give you a head start top-to-toe.

Check out the preferences of the club by asking around. Some established clubs prefer traditional Hollywood western attire and then its acceptable to don all the clothes that we imagine the gunslingers of the old West once wore.

However, it's a different story at new clubs. Line Dancing is a child of the nineties and there's no place for century-old style when fantastic modern-day fashions are freely available. 'We don't merge the new country scene with black and white Western films. These are two separate art forms,' explains Angelique.

Here's Angelique's top seven style suggestions

• Indulge in the really hot fashions. Don't feel compelled to wear gingham or plaid when so many other great materials and patterns are available.

• Leave holsters, guns and tin stars at home for special costume parties.

• Be choosy about skirts. 'Sunset Stampede is not an exercise in cheesecake,' declares Angelique. Only quiet, tiered skirts will do or, if you have the legs for it, go for a mini.

• If you cannot afford a proper hat it's better to be bare-headed than to wear a children's cowboy play-hat from a toy store.

• Never put your jeans inside your boots.

• Abandon your bandanna, it will only make you hot. Keep it in your pocket to wipe off sweat;

• Definitely no spurs, for your own safety as well as others. They can also damage the dance floor;

'There is no need to feel you have to be a Tequila Ted or a Montana Mary and dress incharacter,' says Angelique. 'Just be yourself.'

There are key elements to line dance dress that deserve further explanation...

HATS

Everyone knows what a cowboy hat looks like. They've been seen often enough on films and television, the hallmark of the wild west. The wide-brimmed hat is generally called a Stetson although that is in fact the name of a major brand, just as Ford is one of many makers of cars. Other hat manufacturers include Kangol, Biltmore, Resistol and Dobbs. One of the most distinctive is often referred to as the ten gallon hat but there are many different versions just as there is a range of cars produced by Ford.

But not until you have tried perching a genuine Western style hat on your head can you feel the difference between it and some of the poor hats immitating Stetsons and the like in high street stores.

Hats are made from a blend of wool and beaver fur which together make a heavyweight felt. Of course beavers, large river-bound rodents, are known for their sleek, waterproof coats. These are just the qualities needed in the working man's hat. When buying a Stetson or equivalent look inside the hat band. There you will find an a number of 'X' marks. The more 'X's' in a hat the greater the proportion of beaver fur. Three X and five X hats are commonly found although there are 50 X hats available.

The major disadvantage of wearing bona fide wool and beaver hat for Line Dancing is their weight for the better the hat, the warmer it is. Angelique is under no illusions about why people choose such hats to parade on the dance floor.

'Vanity, there is no other reason,' she admits. 'It's like saying if you can afford a BMW, why buy a Fiesta. These hats are simply better quality.'

WHAT TO WEAR

In America there's no question of settling for second best. 'In the States cheap imitations are play hats, for children only or costume parties,' she explains.

To her line dancing teachers she says: 'Hats are nice, but don't wear one that doesn't suit you. If no hat suits you, forget it. A foolish-looking hat wrecks your credibility.'

The accessible alternative in Britain and Europe is a straw hat. Not only are they much less expensive but they are cooler, too.

JEANS

Still the most acceptable Line Dancing leg gear around, jeans have been the workaday outfits of Americans for years.

The first jeans were made by Levi Strauss (1829-1902) who became of the best-known beneficiaries of Californian gold rush without so much as wielding a shovel.

Levi Strauss was born in Bavaria in 1829. When he came to San Francisco in 1850, he was one of thousands hoping to strike it rich. Trained as a tailor, he had hoped to relieve the flood of prospectors of their money by providing tents and wagon covers. The Forty-Niners, as the gold hunters were known, were slow to appreciate his goods. So instead he used the stout canvas he had brought with him to make especially durable trousers—perfect for miners.

Strauss opened a factory at 98 Battery Street in San Francisco which was by now a boom town with a population which had rocketed from 800 to 55,000 in six short years. He further defined his product by adding copper rivets at the stress points for additional strength. He also switched from canvas to a heavyweight material from France. It came from the town of Nimes and the French term 'de Nimes' soon became shortened to denim. Meanwhile the French word for this material was genes and this, of course, is how the distinctive garment won its name.

Following his rapid success in the rag trade Strauss branched out serving as a director of an insurance company, a utility company, several banks and in a variety of charitable organisations.

The company founded by Levi Strauss is now an international giant. The product which still mirrors his own, is thought of as a rank of excellence in denim trousers everywhere.

Most people possess a pair of jeans. That's another advantage of Line Dancing, you can be at the height of fashion without spending a penny. Angelique and her team from Sunset Stampede wear flattering black jeans when they are on stage.

Another stylish alternative to jeans is leather trousers, although once again these make for a warm evening on the dance floor.

BOOTS

Comfy but never clumpy, cowboy boots are the stock footwear of line dancers everywhere. In America it's possible to buy boots made from an astonishing array of hides. There's python, kangaroo, ostrich, elephant, lizard, goat, shark, calf and buffalo calf.

Look for the number of lines of stitching on cowboy boots to get an idea of its quality. Those stitches are put in place by hand-operated machines. They exist for style and extra strength. The more rows, the better.

Colours vary from the dull to the diabolically bright. It's possible to brighten up a pair of cowboy boots with special straps which clip on around the foot or even boot bracelets.

Angelique dislikes seeing men with jeans inside boots. It goes back to years ago when she visited Montana. Sensitive to her city roots, she was horrified to hear locals brand male visitors with tucked-in jeans as 'drug- store cowboys' meaning they were pale imitations of the real thing. Since that day she has sworn never to give the game away about her own metropolitan background by wearing jeans inside her boots.

Nowadays specially tapered jeans which can be tucked neatly inside fringed dance boots are fashionable for women. But unless jeans are tapered they do not fit neatly inside boots.

'Cowboy boots are a must,' Angelique advises Sunset Stampede teachers. 'They give a more professional, finished look.'

Don't be tempted to substitute trainers for boots. The rubber soles of leisure footwear not only make turns more difficult but introduces some extra unwanted squeaky sound effects, too.

BELTS AND BUCKLES

These days belts do a lot more than simply hold up jeans. They can be eye-catchingly decorative with buckles in the form of a steer's head or a an Indian head-dress. Some buckles are worth thousands of dollars and are more like mini works of art.

NECKWEAR

You've already pocketed the bandanna, that colourful neckerchief so reminiscent of cowboys who might have used them as protection against choking dust during a stampede or even as a mask during a bank raid.

And for those not wanting to copy an old Western theme why not plump for the subtleties of the bollo, a braided leather piece with silver tips or a smart bootlace tie held in place with a decorative fixing?

In the past few years Angelique has seen all manner of fixings ranging from silver and turquoise to a cross-section of highly polished fossilised dinosaur bone, and from 18ct gold bollos with diamonds to simple bears' claws. 'They are truly a work of art,' she admits. Although bollos were originally for men they are now worn by women too.

Angelique's favourite jewellery is influenced heavily by native American traditions. That means plenty of finely worked silver which is attractive without being ostentatious. A leather a bone choker is equally in keeping. There are also some excellent watches, buckles and rings for men but the real Navaho or Zuni jewellery is very expensive.

Here are some more tips for best dressed line dancers:

• Ladies, dress up drab T-shirts with sequins so you can shine on the dance floor;

• Waistcoats are a common accessory. Those with the gambler cut or waistcoats more often seen in snooker halls are both fashionable.

• Men and women can choose between heavy duty cotton, denim or silk shirts. For those who want to sparkle, seek out metal collar tips from specialist stores.

• Even T-shirts with their sleeves cut off can look cool.

• Frills are fine for jackets and shirts.

• Remember, rhinestone are really only for the most confident.

Angelique prefers her dancers to look chic — and that means bold colours and no props. Yet her bottom line on what to wear is refreshingly simple.

'Wear whatever you feel good in,' she states. 'The main aim is to have a great time.'

ETIQUETTE

THE RULES CONCERNING line dancing are few. But they do exist and for very good reasons, namely to avoid close encounters of the physical kind on the dance floor. Nobody wants aggro breaking out during the Armadillo or a rumpus in the Ruby Ruby. Here are a few common-sense measures which will help to keep the peace.

In some clubs the DJ is in charge of the flow of the floor and he or she decides whether or not line dancers will share the floor with couples. With both sets of dancers on the move it is essential to establish some ground rules.

Couples should dance around the outside ring of the hall. Line dancers, if they are permitted on the floor by the DJ at this time, must stay in the middle.

The pairs circuiting the dance floor are obliged to follow the line of dance, which is invariably anti-clockwise. Never dance against the flow.

If the DJ allows couples and line dancers on the floor then line dancers should remember that the outside lanes must be kept clear.

Once given the go-ahead by the DJ couples have right of way and it is the responsibility of line dancers not to impede them.

If possible, start another line rather than join one which will block the progress of those in the outside lane.

When entering or exiting the dance floor wait for an appropriate opening on the floor. It's like joining a main road from a side street. You must yield to those who have the right of way.

In some clubs the DJ is a button-pusher only rather than a vocal instructor. If so it is courteous to follow the dance started by the front line. Beware that some clubs have the floor splintered into groups doing their own thing. For some people that is not as enjoyable as everyone going the same way..

The dance floor is for dancers only so stay away from it unless you are dancing. If you want a chat with an old friend then step to one side.

If you are walking from one side of the dance hall to the other never make your way through the line. Always walk around the edge of the hall or wait until the dance is over before setting off.

Never come on to the dance floor carrying drinks, glasses, cans or cigarettes. Not only are spilled drinks hazardous — other dancers could slip and fall on this unexpected skid pad — but when the bottom of your boots become wet it is difficult to dance. The threat from lighted cigarettes is obvious. Your neighbour in the line does not want holes in their clothes or their skin!

Be mindful of beginners. Remain courteous towards them — and smile. There is nothing more intimidating than a clique of experienced dancers lined up either side of you. Remember, Line Dancing is made for all and everybody has to start somewhere. Even advanced dancers were beginners once — although sometimes they prefer to forget it.

Don't show off by constantly interchanging steps in front of beginners. Too many variations in one familiar routine will put other people off.

Never change steps during a lesson.

Likewise, if the DJ has called a specific dance don't start a different one of your own unless you are occupying an isolated spot off the dance floor. It's unfair on the instructor and the other dancers.

On a crowded floor keep your arms and legs very much to yourself. It may mean toning down an extravagant kick or whirling arm but that's better than giving your neighbour a bloody nose, black eye or knocking a tooth out. Wild leg movements might cause someone to trip or fall.

If the floor is crowded take small steps rather than risk a collision. Remember that you can only move as far as the person next to you.

If you should bump into anyone it is customary to apologise whether it was your fault or not. And should you accidentally spill another's drink replace it immediately. Bear in mind that the aim of Line Dancing is to reduce stress, not increase it.

Don't be tempted to stop dancing in order to teach someone else who is struggling. This is particularly important if the dance floor is busy. Try teaching at the perimeter of the hall rather than in the centre. Of course, it is still important to be helpful to beginners wherever possible — but don't halt a line to do so.

If you are going to start dancing on one of those rare occasions when the floor is empty and the DJ has not called a dance, go to the front so that others can fall into line behind you.

When you visit another club they may do things differently. Obey the rules of the house. Just because it is different doesn't mean it is wrong.

ANGELIQUE SAYS: 'ALL OF THESE RULES ARE DESIGNED TO MAXIMISE OUR PLEASURE AND MINIMISE PROBLEMS WHILE DANCING. PLEASE BE COURTEOUS — AND ENJOY!'

13

THE BASICS

BEFORE EMBARKING on the dances you must know the motions. Then you can launch into all manner of routines without that tell-tale hesitation which make novices stand out like beacons. This detailed photographic glossary reveals all!

Of course, some of the terms used in the description of dances which follows speak for themselves. A clap, kick or hop needs no further explanation here. However, there are Line Dancing terms which you will not immediately recognise. It is those with which we are primarily concerned.

To get the best out of line dancing, it is important to assume the correct posture. Stand up straight with shoulders back and tummies held in. That way you get the pleasure of dancing and the maximum benefit of the exercise it yields.

The upper body remains, for the most part, still during line dancing. Your legs do most of the work. Beginners may feel more comfortable hooking their thumbs into the belt loops of their jeans. When they become more experienced they will experiment using their arms. Choose whichever position feels most natural. Dancers line up facing the instructor when the dances get underway.

When you gain in confidence you might wish to add your own personal flourishes to the dances you have learned, say, a twirling lasso movement with your hand and arm or a clap. This is perfectly acceptable, as long as you remain in time with the music and do not hamper fellow dancers. Some are bold enough to insert a full turn in a backwards walk or a grapevine. Slap your boot or knee any chance you get.

Remember, all these adaptations are fine — provided you don't topple over or distract other dancers. Take small steps when you are launching yourself into a new move. Try practising at home first, in front of a full length mirror, to judge for yourself the final effect.

Each step has a specific number of beats or counts. You will find the number of counts beside each step in the glossary and the count total beside the dances. As you practise the steps it may seem impossible to keep time at first. Don't worry, the music played at line dancing clubs and the words and actions of the instructor will be a tremendous help.

Throughout the glossary we have used the left leg and foot by way of description. However, all steps are quickly adapted to start with either the right foot or the left. Most dances start on the right foot but it isn't always so. The dance instructions or instructor will tell you which direction to follow.

Each dance, through its turns and quarter turns, will change direction. Although you might begin facing the front, with the instructor firmly in your sights, the dance steps may have you swivelling to face the back of the person next to you or the rear wall. Two wall dances face front and rear while four wall dances will be performed to all the walls. When the Line Dancing routine is completed begin it all over again and continue until the music stops.

Angelique has some crucial advice for her line dance students. 'Dance with attitude,' she declares. It's not long before even the rawest rookie dancer knows what she means. To interpret, she wants people to put their heart and soul into the dances. 'Inject a bit of personality, let your hair down — don't be a clone,' Angelique insists.

So don't be afraid to stomp with style, to pivot with panache. Shine as you shuffle and the line shine's with you. As Angelique observes: 'It's just so much fun.'

GLOSSARY

1a

1b

1c

1. BA-DUMP: Otherwise known as a syncopated jump or scooch, this subtle jump was christened the Ba-dump by Sunset Stampede instructor Harley Marshall. 'That's the sound made by a hall full of people doing this step,' she explains. Step forward with the right foot then immediately bring the left foot to join it. Often the ba-dump is followed by a clap. (One count)

2a

2b

2. BUMPS: Put both feet firmly on the floor, thrust the hip to the right or left side. (One count)

3a

3b

3. CHA CHA CHA: Borrowed from the Latin tradition, this step is not meant to cover territory like the shuffle. Change your weight as you step left-right-left on the spot and then rock forward and rock back. (Two counts)

4. CAMEL WALK: Step forward with the left leg, then roll your hips as you bring your right foot forward to meet the left, keeping it close to the floor as you do so. (two counts)

4a

4b

4c

5. CHARLESTON: Once again, this is a recycled step, this time from the Roaring Twenties. Step forward on the left foot, kick with the right foot, step back on right and then point behind with the left toe. When you become an accomplished line dancer it is possible to turn during the Charleston. (four counts)

5a

5b

5c

5d

6. COASTER STEP: Step back on the left foot, bring your right foot next to it then the left foot goes forward once more. (two counts)

6a

6b

6c

GLOSSARY

7a

7b

7. GIANT STEP OR SLIDE: Take your time with this one. Stride out with one foot, then pull your other leg forward to meet it, sliding it along the ground. (Four counts)

7c

7d

8a

8b

8. GRAPEVINE: This is one of the fundamental steps of line dancing. You've probably seen a similar motion during traditional Greek dances. A right grapevine means a step to the right, cross your left foot behind the right foot, step with your right foot to the right side and bring the left to join it. A left grapevine is, of course, the same but in reverse (Four counts).

Longer grapevines are sometimes required, those with six or eight counts. Begin as you would for a normal grapevine, and continue by crossing your left leg in front of the right. Alternate the crossing legs thereafter.

8c

8d

8e

9. ROLLING GRAPEVINE: As you become more skilled you may wish to introduce a turn during the grapevine. Using the same number of steps but this time angling your feet, rotate your body 360 degrees throughout the movement. (Four counts)

9a

9b

9c

9d

9c

9d

9e

10. GRINDS: With your feet on the floor sway your hips from one side to the other. The Silent Cowboys have modified this step, especially for fellas. With both hands on their hats they grind forward and backwards instead of side to side. (One count)

10a

10b

GLOSSARY

11a

11b

11. HEELS: Put out your heel diagonally, then return to standing. The instructor will dictate whether the dance demands a left or right heel. (Two counts)

12a

12b

12c

12. HEEL SWIVELS: With your weight forward onto the toes, swivel heels to one side then the other, keeping your toes still. Toe swivels are in reverse. The weight stays back on the heels and your toes swivel from side to side. (One count)

12d

13a

13b

13c

13. HIP THRUST: With legs apart, bend your knees then thrust the pelvis forward while pulling the elbows back. The shoulders stay still throughout. (One count per thrust)

20

14. HITCHES: Lift knee. (One count)

15. HITCH TURNS: Lift knee and change direction in either a quarter or a half turn. (One count)

16a

16b

16. HOOK: Put your right heel out at 45 degrees, hitch your right ankle up in front of the left knee. Bring the heel down and finally in. (Four counts)

16c

GLOSSARY

17a

17b

17c

17d

17. JAZZ BOX: Start by crossing your right foot over the left, step back on the left, step right to the side then close the left foot to the right. This step can be done in reverse, too, starting with left over right. During this step your feet have marked the four corners of a square. Think of the box dance closely associated with *Dance On* by the Shadows during the '60s and you will instantly visualise this step. Once again, it is possible to introduce a turn into a jazz box. Cross your right foot over the left, step back with the left and begin a quarter turn to the right. Usually there are two jazz boxes together in line dances. (Four counts)

18a   18b   18c

18.* KICK BALL CHANGE: Kick forward with your right foot on the first count, then step down on the ball of your left foot and swiftly transfer your weight back to the right foot. (Two counts)

*These steps are relevant to *both* left and right foot first, depending on the dance — your instructor will tell you which to use.

19.* KICK BALL POINT: Kick forward with your right foot on the first count, then step down on the ball of your left foot as above. Finish by pointing your left foot to the side. (Two counts)

19a

19b

19c

20. KNEE SWINGS: Lift your heel then swing that knee out and in again. (Two counts)

*These steps are relevant to *both* left and right foot first, depending on the dance — your instructor will tell you which to use.

20a

20b

GLOSSARY

21a

21b

21. KNEE ROLLS: Lift your heel then make a circular motion with the knee. (Two counts)

22. PIGEON TOES: Also known as buttermilks and split heels, it's a familiar movement. With body weight on the balls of your feet, spread your heels apart and then bring them back together. (Two counts)

23. POINT TO THE SIDE: A self-explanatory movement, point your toe to the side then return to a standing position. (Two counts)

24. SAILOR STEP: Cross your left foot behind the right, bring your right foot beside the left, then step slightly to the left with your left foot, going backwards and making an 'S' shape on the floor. (Two counts)

24a

24b

24c

24d

24e

24f

25. SCOOT: Like a hitch, the knee is lifted. In that position you cover ground by taking small hops forward on the floor-bound foot. (One count per scoot)

25a

25b

25c

26. SHIMMIES: Shake the shoulders, stepping out at the same time with arms by your sides. This is generally thought of as a ladies-only movement and men usually substitute a hip thrust. (As many shakes as possible per count)

26a

26b

26c

GLOSSARY

27a

27b

27. SHUFFLE: Step forward on one foot, bring the other one alongside, then step forward once more, on the same foot that your started with. There are right shuffles and left shuffles, denoting which foot you begin on, and also backwards shuffles. It's three steps in two counts. (Two counts)

27c

28. STEP SLIDE: Simply step forward, and then slide the other leg to meet the first. (Two counts)

28a

28b

28c

29a

29b

29. STEP PIVOT: Step forward on to the left foot, turn around on the balls of your feet towards the right to face the opposite direction, keeping your feet on ground. Try this and you will find it impossible to turn the wrong way without moving your feet. Quarter pivots follow the same principle but the turn is 90 degrees instead of 180 degrees. (Two counts)

30. STOMP: Stamp your foot down. This step is invaluable for noise effect! (one count)

31a

31b

31. STRUTS: Step out with the left heel on the first count, drop the left toe on the second count. Repeat with the right. This is basically walking with a heel-toe action. (two counts per foot)

31c

31d

32. TOE FANS: Keep your heels together and fan your toes out. You might have to fan using the left foot, the right foot or both. Return to a standing position. (two counts)

32a

32b

32c

GLOSSARY

33. TOE BEHIND: Point your toe behind, right or left as required, then return to standing. (Two counts)

34. UNWIND: When your legs are crossed keep body weight on the balls of feet and turn body, 'unwinding' our legs. (One count)

34a

34b

34c

35. WEAVE: Take a deep breath because this is a long one! Cross your right foot over the left, step back on the left foot, step back on the right, take your left foot across the right, step back on the right, bring left foot next to right. (Six counts)

35a

35b

35c

At last you're ready to put the steps to music and discover the thrills of line dancing!

Angelique has put together these easy-to-follow dance sheets to get you started.

The movements have been broken down into simple stages — all you have to do is put them together again. The sheets tell you not only how many counts in each dance but also how many counts in each separate step. Every line is, generally speaking, worth one count.

Keep your glossary handy. You will probably want to refer back to it and check out the more detailed descriptions of the steps. After a bit of practice you will merely glance at the step title and launch into it without a second thought. When you get to the end of the sequence, start all over again. Good luck . . . and happy dancing!

& = half count

Flick = Bring leg up behind

Lunge = Cross one foot over the other and dip

CC = Counter clockwise

Brush/Scuff = move foot forward and scuff floor, weight remains on other leg

Touch = Bringing foot back to place, weight remains on other leg

LOD = Line of Dance

Top, *Middle* or *Bottom* show where the explanatory photos are located

35d   35e   35f

TOO MUCH FUN

Music: Too Much Fun *by Daryle Singletary* **Choreographer:** *Gloria Johnson, Florida* **Walls:** Two **Counts:** 32

(Eight counts)
(Top) 1. POINT AND JUMP
Point right toe to the right:
Jump, and point left toe out to left:
Jump, and point right toe out to right:
Clap, jump, and point left toe out to left:
Jump, and point right toe out to right:
Jump, and point left toe out to left:
Clap.

(Eight counts)
2. CHARLESTON
Step forward on left:
Kick right foot forward:
Step back on right foot:
Touch left toe behind:
Step forward on left foot with a quarter turn to the left:
Kick right foot forward:
Step back on right foot:
Step left foot behind (weight on left foot).

(Four counts)
(Middle) 3. RIGHT GRAPEVINE
Step right:
Left foot behind:
Step right to the side:
Touch left next to right.

(Four counts)
4. ROLLING LEFT GRAPEVINE
Step left (angling foot):
Swing right foot around, turn:
Swing left foot around, continue turn and finish facing original direction:
Touch right beside left.

(Four counts)
5. KICK BALL CHANGES
Kick right foot forward:
Step down on the ball of right foot:
Transfer weight to the left foot:
Kick right foot forward:
Step down on the ball of right foot:
Transfer weight to the left foot.

(Two counts)
6. STEP AND TURN
Step forward on right foot:
Make a quarter turn to the left on the balls of feet.

(Two counts)
(Bottom) 7. STOMP AND CLAP
Stomp right foot next to left and clap:
Stomp right foot next to left and clap.

30

ALLEY CAT

Music: Water to a Drowning Man *by Lee Roy Parnell.* C-O-U-N-T-R-Y *by Joe Diffie.* I Feel Lucky *by Mary Chapin Carpenter* **Choreographer:** *Unknown* **Walls:** *Four* **Counts:** *68*

(Four counts)
1. HEELS (*Top*)
Tap right heel forward:
Return to standing position:
Tap right heel forward:
Return to standing position.

(Four counts)
2. HEEL SWIVELS
Swivel both heels to the right:
Return:
Swivel both heels to the right:
Return.

(Four counts)
3. HEELS
Tap left heel forward:
Return:
Tap left heel forward:
Return.

(Four counts)
4. HEEL SWIVELS
Swivel both heels to the right:
Return:
Swivel both heels to the right:
Return.

(Eight counts)
5. CAMEL WALK (*Middle*)
Step forward with left leg:
Slide right foot to meet left leg, rolling hips:
(— try making a lasso movement with your arm here):
REPEAT THREE MORE TIMES.

(Eight counts)
6. STEP BACK CLAP (*Bottom*)
Step back on right, slightly pivoting to the right:
Bring left foot together with right and clap:
Step back on left foot, slightly pivoting to the left:
Bring right foot together and clap:
REPEAT ALL OF THE ABOVE.

(Sixteen counts)
7. SHIMMY (women) / HIP THRUSTS (men)
Step to the right and shimmy/hip thrust:
Slide left foot to meet right foot and clap:
REPEAT THESE TWO THEN:
Step to the left and shimmy/hip thrust:
Slide right foot to meet left foot and clap:
REPEAT THESE TWO.

ALLEY CAT

(Four counts)
(Top) 8. **KICK BALL CHANGE**
Kick right foot forward:
Step down on the ball of right foot:
Transfer weight to the left foot:
(Remember, each kick ball
change is two counts, the count
is one and two):
Repeat the above.

(Four counts)
9. **STEP AND PIVOT TURN**
Step forward on right foot:
Bring left together:
Place left foot to the side:
Pivot a quarter turn to the left.

(Eight counts)
10. **LEFT GRAPEVINE**
Step left:
Cross right foot behind left:
Step left to the side:
Finish with a stomp. Step right:
Cross left foot behind right:
Step right to the side:
Finish with a stomp.

(Four counts)
*(Bottom)*11. **STEP BACKWARDS**
Step back left:
Step back right:
Step back left:
Stomp right next to left.

HIGH TEST LOVE

Music: High Test Love *by Scooter Lee.* Corridor 38 *by Union Street*   **Choreographer:** *Max Perry, Danbury.*
Walls: *Four*   **Counts:** *32*

(Eight counts)
1. **CAJUN SHUFFLES WITH HITCH** *(Top)*
Step forward on left, slide right to meet left:
Step forward on left, hitch right while scooting forward on left:
Step forward on right, slide left to meet right:
Step forward on right, hitch right while scooting forward on left.

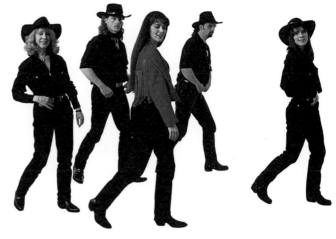

(Four counts)
2. **STEP BACK, SCOOT** *(Middle)*
Step back on left, hitch right while scooting back on left:
Step back on right:
Hitch left while scooting back on right.

(Four counts)
3. **HOOK AND SLAP** *(Bottom)*
Step left, step right (feet apart):
Shift weight to left foot:
Hook right ankle behind left knee and slap with left hand.

(12 counts)
4. **SIDE STEPS WITH HITCHES**
Step right, step left next to right:
Step right, hitch left while scooting on right:
Step left, step right next to left:
Step left, hitch right while scooting on left:
Step right, step left next to right:
Step right, hitch left and scoot on right.

(Four counts)
5. **THREE QUARTER TURN TO THE LEFT**
Step forward left, beginning turn:
Step slightly back on right, continue turn:
Step forward left, continue turn:
Step slightly back on right, continue turn:
(Finish with weight on right).

FOOT BOOGIE

Music: Shine Them Buckles *by the Bellamy Brothers.* Boogie 'til the Cows Come Home *by Clay Walker*
Choreographer: *Unknown* **Walls:** *Two* **Counts:** *32*

T(Eight counts)
(Top) 1. **TOE FANS**
Keep heels together and fan right toe out:
Return:
Keep heels together and fan right toe out:
Return:
Keep heels together and fan left toe out:
Return:
Keep heels together and fan left toe out:
Return:
(Every toe fan is worth two counts — see Glossary).

(Eight counts)
2. **TOE FANS AND HEEL SWIVELS**
With weight on left leg, toe fan with right foot:
Heel swivel right:
Heel swivel back to place:
Toe fan back to original standing point:
With weight on right leg, toe fan with left foot:
Heel swivel left:
Heel swivel back:
Toe fan back to original standing point.

(Four counts)
(Middle) 3. **TOES AND HEELS**
Toe fan with both feet — toes away from each other:
Heel swivels apart with both feet:
Toe fan back to place:
Heel swivels back to place.

(12 counts)
(Bottom) 4. **STEP SLIDES**
Step forward on right:
Slide left foot to meet it —
keeping it locked behind the right:
Step forward on right:
Hitch up left knee:
Step forward on left:
Slide right foot to meet it —
keeping it locked behind the left:
Step forward on left:
Hitch right knee and make half turn to the left —
facing rear wall:
Step forward on right:
Slide left foot to meet it:
Step forward on right:
Stomp left foot.

COWBOY STRUT

Music: Would I *by Randy Travis.* Slow Me Down *by Shelby Lynne.* Anyway the Wind Blows *by Brother Phelps*
Choreographer: Unknown **Walls:** *Two* **Counts:** *32*

(Eight counts)
1. HEEL SWIVELS *(Top)*
Swivel right heel to right and return to centre:
Swivel left heel to left and return to centre:
REPEAT ALL OF THE ABOVE.

(Four counts)
2. TAPS
Tap your right foot in front twice:
Tap your left toe behind twice.

(Two counts)
3. HEELS *(Middle)*
Tap your right heel in front and clap.

(Two counts)
4. TAP *(Middle Below)*
Tap your right toe behind once, then clap.

(Eight counts)
5. HEEL-TOE STRUTS
Step on right heel:
Tap down right toe:
Step on left heel:
Tap down on left toe:
REPEAT ALL OF THE ABOVE.

(Eight counts)
6. TURNING JAZZ BOX *(Bottom)*
Step forward on right foot:
Step backwards on to the left foot, beginning a right turn:
Step to the right with right foot —
you are now facing the right wall:
REPEAT ALL OF THE ABOVE —
you are now facing the back wall.

35

HAUNTED HEART

Music: Haunted Heart *by Sammy Kershaw.* What You Don't Know *by Jon Randall* **Choreographer:** *Tony Kwiatkowski and Donna Ziemer* **Walls:** *Unknown* **Counts:** 64

(four counts)
(Top) 1. STRUT
Right heel forward:
Touch down with right toe:
Left heel forward:
Touch down with left toe.

(two counts)
2. STEPS
Step forward with right foot:
Step forward with left foot.

(four counts)
3. STRUT
Right heel forward:
Touch down with right toe:
Left heel forward:
Touch down with left toe.

(Two counts)
4. STEPS
Step forward with right foot:
Step forward with left foot.

(Four counts)
5. STRUT
Right heel forward:
Touch down with right toe:
Left heel forward:
Touch down with left toe.

(four counts)
6. STEPS
Cross right foot over left and step down:
Hold for one beat:
Step back on to left foot:
Hold for one beat.

(12 counts)
(Bottom) 7. STEP AND CLAP
Step back diagonally on right, touch floor with left foot, clap at the same time:
Step back diagonally on left, touch floor with right foot, clap at the same time:
Step back diagonally on right, touch floor with left foot, clap at the same time:
Step back diagonally on left, touch floor with right foot, clap at the same time:
Step back diagonally on right, touch floor with left foot, clap at the same time:
Step back diagonally on left, touch floor with right foot, clap at the same time.

(Four counts)
8. HEELS *(Top)*
Tap right heel diagonally forward, hold for one beat:
Tap right heel diagonally forward, hold for one beat.

(Four counts)
9. STEPS
Step right foot behind left:
Step to the left on left foot:
Step right foot across left:
Pause for one beat.

(Four counts)
10. HEELS
Tap left heel forward diagonally, hold for one beat:
Tap left heel forward diagonally, hold for one beat.

(Four counts)
11. STEPS *(Middle)*
Step left foot behind right:
Step to the right on right foot:
Step left foot across right:
Pause for one beat.

(Four counts)
12. HEELS
Tap right heel forward diagonally, hold for one beat:
Tap right heel forward diagonally, hold for one beat.

(Four counts)
13. STEPS
Step right foot behind left:
Step to the left on left foot:
Step right foot across left:
Pause for one beat.

(Four counts)
14. HEELS
Tap left heel forward diagonally, hold for one beat:
Tap left heel forward diagonally, hold for one beat.

(Four counts)
15. STEP AND TURN *(Bottom)*
Step left behind right:
Step to the right while making a quarter turn to the right:
Step left foot next to right foot:
Pause for one beat.

THE WALK

Music: No One Needs To Know *by Shania Twain* Laid Back Stone Cold *by Michelle Wright*
Choreographer: *Unknown* **Walls:** *Four* **Counts:** *40*

(Eight counts)
(Top 1. RIGHT KNEE SWINGS AND HOOK
Swing right knee out, in, out, in:
Hook with right ankle just below left knee.

(Eight counts)
2. **LEFT KNEE SWINGS AND HOOK**
Swing left knee out, in, out, in:
Hook with left ankle over right knee.

(Eight counts)
(Middle) 3. **RIGHT AND LEFT HEEL TAPS**
Right heel (diagonally) forward:
Return:
Left heel forward:
Return;
Right heel forward:
Return:
Left heel forward:
Return.

(Eight counts)
4. **JAZZ BOXES**
Cross right foot over left:
Step back on left:
Step right to the side:
Bring left together:
REPEAT ALL OF THE ABOVE.

(Four counts)
(Bottom) 5. **ROLLING LEFT GRAPEVINE**
Step left and begin to make a half turn left (CC):
Continue to make a half turn left on right foot (CC):
Make a quarter turn left on left foot:
Touch right foot together.

(Four counts)
6. **RIGHT GRAPEVINE**
Step right:
Cross left foot behind right:
Step right to the side:
Finish with a stomp.

CONFUSION

Music: Let's Go To Vegas *by Faith Hill.* Old Enough to Know Better *by Wade Hayes*   ***Choreographer:*** *Unkown*   ***Walls:*** *Two*   ***Counts:*** *46*

(Four counts)
1. HEELS *(Top*
Tap right heel forward:
Return to standing position:
REPEAT ALL OF THE ABOVE.

(Four counts)
2. HEEL SWIVELS
Swivel both heels to the right:
Return:
REPEAT ALL OF THE ABOVE.

(Four counts)
3. HEELS
Tap left heel forward:
Return to standing position:
REPEAT ALL OF THE ABOVE.

(Four counts) *(Middle Top)*
4. HEEL SWIVELS
Swivel both heels to the left:
Return:
REPEAT ALL OF THE ABOVE.

(Four counts)
5. HEELS
Tap right heel forward:
Return to standing position:
REPEAT ALL OF THE ABOVE.

(Four counts)
6. TAP
Tap right toe behind:
Return to standing position:
REPEAT ALL OF THE ABOVE.

(Two counts)
7. HEELS
Tap right heel forward:
Return to standing position.

(Two counts) *(Middle Below)*
8. HEELS
Tap left heel forward:
Return to standing position.

(Two counts)
9. HEELS
Tap right heel forward:
Return to standing position.

(Two counts)
10. HEELS
Tap left heel forward:
Return to standing position.

(Two counts)
11. STEP PIVOT
Step forward on right foot:
Pivot 180 degrees — finish facing rear wall.

(Two counts)
12. SHUFFLE *(Bottom)*
Shuffle forward on right foot — right, left, right:
Shuffle forward on left foot — left, right, left —
remember, the count for a shuffle is one and two.

COWGIRL TWIST

Music: Honky Tonkin's What I Do Best *by Marty Stuart and Travis Tritt* What the Cowgirls Do *by Vince Gill*
Choreographer: *Unknown* **Walls:** *Four* **Counts:** *32*

(Eight counts)
(Top) 1. **STRUTS**
Step out with right heel:
Touch down with right toe:
Step out with left heel:
Touch down with left toe:
Step out with right heel:
Touch down with right toe:
Step out with left heel:
Touch down with left toe.

(Four counts)
2. **WALK**
Walk backwards, right, left, right, left next to right.

(Four counts)
(Bottom) 3. **HEEL SWIVELS**
Swivel both heels left:
Swivel both toes left:
Swivel both heels left:
Clap.

(Four counts)
4. **HEEL SWIVELS**
Swivel both heels right:
Swivel both toes right:
Swivel both heels right:
Clap.

(Four counts)
5. HEEL SWIVELS *(Top)*
Swivel heels left and clap:
Swivel heels right and clap.

(four counts)
6. HEEL SWIVELS *(Middle)*
Swivel heels left:
Swivel heels right:
Swivel heels left:
Swivel heels centre.

(Two counts)
7. STEP
Step forward on right foot and hold.

(two counts)
8. PIVOT *(Bottom)*
Pivot one quarter turn to the left and hold.

ROCKING REBEL

Music: *That's My Story by Collin Raye*   **Choreographer:** *Linda DeFord*   **Walls:** *Four*   **Counts:** *32*

(Eight counts)
(Top) 1. **SIDE SHUFFLES WITH ROCK BACK**
Shuffle to the right — right, left, right:
Rock back on left foot, rock forward on right:
Shuffle to the left — left, right, left:
Rock back on right foot, rock forward on left.

(Four counts)
(Middle) 2. **FORWARD SHUFFLE AND HALF PIVOT TURN**
Shuffle forward on the right foot — right, left, right:
Step left foot forward, pivot half turn to the right —
keep weight on right foot with stomp, facing back
wall.

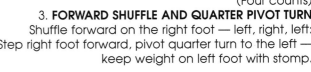

(Four counts)
3. **FORWARD SHUFFLE AND QUARTER PIVOT TURN**
Shuffle forward on the right foot — left, right, left:
Step right foot forward, pivot quarter turn to the left —
keep weight on left foot with stomp.

(Four counts)
(Bottom) 4. **FORWARD SHUFFLE AND HALF PIVOT TURN**
Shuffle forward on the right foot — right, left, right:
Step left foot forward, pivot half turn to the right —
keep weight on right foot with stomp.

(Four counts)
5. FORWARD SHUFFLE AND QUARTER PIVOT TURN *(Top)*
Shuffle forward on the right foot — left, right, left:
Step right foot forward, pivot quarter turn to the left —
keep weight on left foot with stomp, facing back wall.

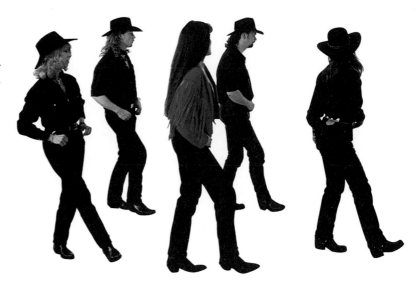

(Three counts)
6. QUARTER PIVOT TURN AND STOMP
Step forward on the right foot:
Pivot a quarter turn to the left:
Stomp right foot next to left.

(Three counts)
7. KICKS
Kick left foot forward:
Step backward on left foot — behind right:
Kick right foot forward.

(Two counts)
8. CROSS AND UNWIND *(Bottom)*
Cross right foot over left:
Unwind a half turn:
The dance finishes with dancers facing the original left
wall.

LOUISIANA HOT SAUCE

Music: My Little Jalapeno *by Scooter Lee*   **Choreographers:** *J. Brady, G. Elliott, M. Perry, J. Thompson.*
Walls: *Two*   **Counts:** *32*

(Four counts)
(Top) 1. **STRUTS AND HEEL DROPS**
Left heel forward, drop left toe and lift heel: (illustrated)
Tap left heel twice — finish with weight on left:
Right heel forward, drop right toe and lift heel:
Tap right heel twice — weight finishes on right.
— One & two & three & four —

(Two counts)
(Middle) 2. **CROSS, UNWIND, HEEL SWIVEL AND CLAP**
Cross left over right leg, Unwind in a half turn towards the right:
Finish facing back wall with weight on the left foot.

(Two counts)
(Bottom) 3. **HEEL SWIVELS AND CLAP**
Swivel both heels right, left, right: (illustrated).
Clap hands.
— One & two & —

(Four counts)
4. **FORWARD 'CAJUN' JOGS AND CLAP**
With weight on toes, step forward left, right, left as per cha cha:
Hitch up right knee and take a small hop on left, clapping hands:
With weight on toes step forward right, left, right as per cha cha:
Hitch up left knee and take a small hop on right, clapping hands.
— One & two & three & four —

(Four counts)
5. BACK HITCHES, FORWARD STOMP *(Top)*
Step back on left, slightly crossing behind:
Take a small hop on left, hitching right knee:
Step back on right, slightly crossing behind:
Rock back on ball of left:
Stomp right forward, on diagonal. Hold for one count, weight finishes on right.
— One & two & three & four —

(Eight counts)
6.CROSS ROCKS AND QUARTER TURN — LEFT *(Middle)*
Cross left over right, bend knees:
Rock back on right:
Small step with left foot to left side:
— that's one & two —
Cross right over left — bend knees:
Rock back on left:
Small step with right foot to right side:
— three & four —
Cross left over right, bend knees:
Rock back on left:
Small step left, turning a quarter turn to the left:
— five and six —
Continue left turn with right slightly behind left:
Step on right, step forward on left, turning left:
— (& seven —
Step on right, step forward on left, completing full turn.
— & eight —

(Eight counts)
7. CROSS ROCKS AND QUARTER TURN — RIGHT *(Bottom)*
Cross right over left, bend knees:
Rock back on left:
Small step with right foot to right side:
— that's one & two —
Cross left over right, bend knees:
Rock back on right:
Small step with left foot to left side:
— three & four —
Cross right over left, bend knees:
Rock back on right:
Small step right, turning a quarter turn to the right:
— five & six —
Continue right turn with left slightly behind right:
Step on left, step forward on right, turning right:
— & seven —
Step on left, step forward on right, completing full turn.
— & eight —

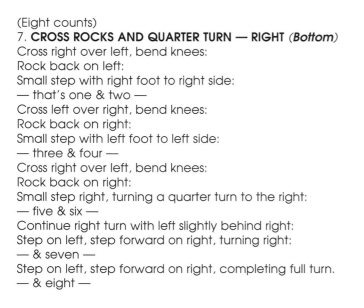

COPPERHEAD ROAD

Music: Copperhead Road *by Steve Earle*   *Choreographer:* Max Perry, Danbury   *Walls:* Four   *Counts:* 24

(Four counts)
(Top) 1. **HEELS AND TOE BEHIND**
Right heel forward and return:
Point left toe behind and return.

(One count)
2. **TOE BEHIND**
Cross right toe behind.

(Three counts)
(Middle) 3. **RIGHT GRAPEVINE**
Step right, cross left foot behind:
Step right and make a quarter turn to the right.
— Finish facing right wall —

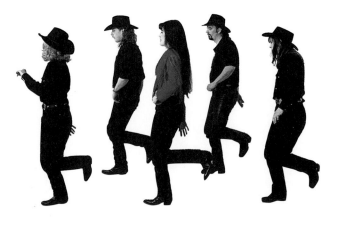

(Two counts)
(Bottom) 4. **SCOOT**
With weight on right foot, scoot to the left twice.

46

(Four counts)
5. LEFT GRAPEVINE
Step left, cross right foot behind:
Step left, finish with a right flick:
Slap inside right foot.

(Four counts)
6. RIGHT GRAPEVINE *(Top)*
Step right, cross left foot behind:
Step right, finish with a left flick.

(Four counts)
7. WALK BACK AND HITCH *(Middle)*
Walk back left, right, left:
Finish with right hitch.

(Two counts)
8. STOMPS *(Bottom)*
Stomp right, stomp left.

FALLSVIEW ROCK

Music: *You Win My Love by Shania Twain. Swingin' on My Baby's Chain by Phillip Claypool. Heart's Desire by Lee Roy Parnell* **Choreographer:** *Unknown* **Walls:** *Two* **Counts:** *32*

(Eight counts)
1. SAILOR SHUFFLES
— the count is 'one & two' —
Cross left behind right:
Step right in place:
Step left next to right:
Cross right behind left:
Step left in place:
Step right next to left:
REPEAT ALL OF THE ABOVE.

(Two counts)
(Top) **2. TWO LEFT KICKS**
Kick left foot forward twice.

(Two counts)
(Bottom) **3. COASTER STEP**
— the count is 'one & two' —
Step back on left:
Step right next to left:
Step forward on left.
— you can substitute a cha cha.

(Two counts)
4. KICKS
Kick right foot forward twice.

48

(Two counts)
5. COASTER STEP *(Top)*
— the count is 'one &two'
Step back on right:
Step left next to right:
Step forward on right.
— you can substitute a cha cha.

(Eight counts)
6. HIP BUMPS *(Middle)*
Step forward on left and bump left hip twice:
Step forward on right and bump right hip twice:
Step forward on left and bump left hip twice:
Step forward on right and bump right hip twice.

(Four counts)
7. STOMP, KICK AND TURN
Stomp left foot forward, kick right out to right side:
Cross over left:
With weight on balls of feet, unwind half turn to left:
Finish with weight on right foot.

(Four counts)
8. SHUFFLES *(Bottom)*
— the count is 'one &two'
Left shuffle forward — left, right, left:
Right shuffle forward — right, left, right.

MIDNIGHT WALTZ

Music: Children *by The Mavericks.* Dreamin' My Dreams *by Collin Raye*   **Choreographer:** *Jo Thompson, Nashville*
Walls: Four   **Counts:** 48

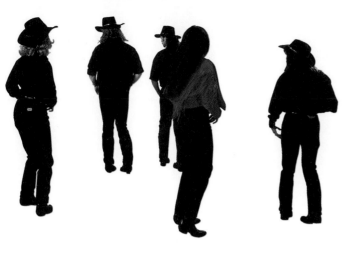

(12 counts)
— waltz rhythm 'one, two, three one' —
(Top) CROSS OVERS AND HALF RIGHT TURN
Cross left foot over right, step right to the side, step left next to right:
Cross right over left, step left to the side and begin half right turn:
(illustrated) Step right next to left finishing half right turn:
— you are now facing rear wall —
REPEAT ALL OF THE ABOVE:
— you are now facing original front wall —

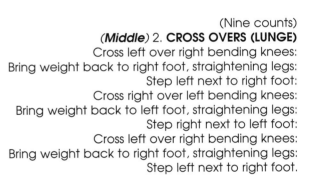

(Nine counts)
(Middle) 2. CROSS OVERS (LUNGE)
Cross left over right bending knees:
Bring weight back to right foot, straightening legs:
Step left next to right foot:
Cross right over left bending knees:
Bring weight back to left foot, straightening legs:
Step right next to left foot:
Cross left over right bending knees:
Bring weight back to right foot, straightening legs:
Step left next to right foot.

(Three counts)
(Bottom) 3. LEFT GRAPEVINE
Cross right over left:
Step left to the side:
Cross right behind left.

(Six counts)
4. GIANT STEP/SLIDE LEFT AND RIGHT
Take a large step to the left and slowly slide right foot
to meet left:
Take a large step to the right and slowly slide left foot
to meet right.

(12 counts)
STEP SWING AND HALF LEFT TURN *(Top)*
Step forward on left, swing right leg forward and hold
for one count:
Step back on right foot, beginning half left turn:
Step left, step right:
— you are now facing back wall —
Step forward on left, swing right leg forward and hold
for one count:
Step back on right foot, beginning half left turn:
Step left, step right.
— you are now facing front wall.

(Six counts)
BALANCE FORWARD AND
BACK WITH TURN *(Bottom)*
Step left foot forward while making quarter turn:
Step right beside left, step left beside right:
Step right back, step left beside right, step right in
place.

FAST AS YOU

Music: Fast As You *by Dwight Yoakam* **Choreographer:** *Unknown* **Walls:** *Four* **Counts:** *40*

(Four counts)
1. RIGHT GRAPEVINE
Step right, cross left foot behind right:
Step right, bring left foot together with right.

(Four counts)
(Top) 2. POINT AND JUMP
Point left toe to the side then jump, switching feet:
Point right toe to the side:
Jump, switching feet:
And point left toe to the side, then clap.

(Four counts)
3. LEFT GRAPEVINE
Step left, cross right foot behind left:
Step left, bring right foot together with left.

(Four counts)
(Middle) 4. POINT AND JUMP
Point right toe to the side then jump, switching feet:
Point left toe to the side:
Jump, switching feet:
And point right toe to the side, then clap.

(Four counts)
(Bottom) 5. HIP BUMPS
Twice forward, twice backwards.

(Four counts)
6. **HEEL SWIVELS** *(Top)*
With weight on toes, swivel both heels to the right, left, right and left and right;
— the count is 'one, two, three & four' —

(Eight counts)
7. **CHARLESTON**
Kick right leg forward:
Return:
Point left toe back:
Return:
Kick right leg forward:
Return:
Point left toe back:
Return:
Finish with weight on left.

(Four counts)
8. **SCOOT AND STOMP** *(Middle)*
Scoot forward on left foot twice:
Stomp right foot then left foot.

(Four counts)
9. **HOOK, TURN AND STOMP** *(Bottom)*
Hook right foot behind left ankle:
Make a quarter turn to the left:
Finish facing left wall:
Stomp right foot twice.

CALIFORNIA STOMP

Music: Hardcore Troubadour *by Steve Earle* Don't Ask Me No Questions *by Travis Tritt*
Choreographer: *Unknown* **Walls:** *Two* **Counts:** *64*

(Eight counts)
(Top) 1. **STOMP AND CLAP AND SHUFFLE**
Stomp forward on right:
Return and clap:
Stomp forward on right:
Return and clap:
Shuffle in place, right, left, right:
— count 'one & two' —
TOP PIC Stomp forward on left:
Step left back to place and clap.

(Eight counts)
(Middle) 2. **SHUFFLE, ROCK BACK**
Shuffle left — left, right, left —
— count 'one & two' —
Rock back on right:
Rock forward on left:
Shuffle right — right, left, right —
Rock back on left:
Rock forward on right.

(Eight counts)
(Bottom) 3. **SHUFFLE, PIVOT, SHUFFLE**
Left shuffle forward, left, right, left:
— count 'one & two' —
Step forward on right, pivot half turn left:
Finish facing rear wall with weight on left foot:
Right shuffle forward, right, left, right:
Left shuffle forward, left, right, left.

(Eight counts)
4. **STOMP AND CLAP AND SHUFFLE**
Stomp forward on right:
Return and clap:
Stomp forward on right:
Return and clap:
Shuffle in place, right, left, right.
(count 'one and two') Stomp forward on left;
Step left back to place and clap;

54

Eight counts)
5. LEFT AND RIGHT ROLLING GRAPEVINE AND CLAP (*Top*)
Step left and begin making a full left turn:
Keep turning with each step until you face the rear wall once more:
— Left, right, left, stomp right and clap —
Step right and begin making a full right turn:
Keep turning with each step until you face the rear wall once more.
— Right, left, right, stomp left and clap —

(Eight counts)
6. BA-DUMPS AND CROSS (*Middle*)
Count: — & one, & two, & three, four —
Left foot steps left, right foot steps right (ba-dump):
Cross legs, left leg in front, right leg behind:
Left foot steps left, right foot steps right (ba-dump):
Clap:
Left foot steps left, right foot steps right (ba-dump):
Cross legs, right leg in front, left leg behind:
Clap.
— Finish with weight on left foot —

(Eight counts)
7. RIGHT AND LEFT SIDE STEP (*Bottom*)
Step right, slide left together:
Step right, slide left together:
Step left, slide right together:
Step left, slide right together.

(Eight counts)
8. KICK BALL CHANGE AND PIVOT
Kick ball change with right foot:
Step forward on right:
Pivot half left turn:
— You are now facing original front wall —
Kick ball change with right foot:
Step forward on right:
Pivot half left turn.
— You are now facing rear wall —

SWAMP THANG

Music: Swamp Thang *by The Grid* **Choreographer:** Dan Perry **Walls:** Four **Counts:** 40

(Four counts)
(Top) 1. **ROCK AND COASTER STEP**
Rock forward on left foot:
Step in place with right:
Step back on left:
Bring right together:
Step forward on left:
— the count is 'one, two, three & four' —
You can replace the coaster step with the cha cha.

(Four counts)
2. **ROCK AND COASTER STEP**
Rock forward on right foot:
Step in place with left:
Step back on right:
Bring left together:
Step forward on right.
— the count is 'one, two, three & four' —

(Four counts)
(Middle) 3. **ROCK AND SHUFFLE**
Rock step to the left with left foot:
Step in place with right:
Shuffle left, right, left:
— the count is 'one, two, three & four' —

(Four counts)
4. **ROCK AND CHA CHA**
Rock step to the right with right foot:
Step in place with left:
Cha cha right, left, right.
— the count is 'one, two, three & four' —

(Four counts)
5. **LEFT GRAPEVINE**
Step to the left:
Cross right behind left:
Step to the left:
Step together with right.

(Four counts)
6. SHUFFLE AND ROCK STEP
Shuffle left, right, left:
Rock step back with right:
Step in place with left foot.
— the count is 'one & two, three, four' —

(Four counts)
7. RIGHT GRAPEVINE *(Top)*
Step to the right:
Cross left behind right:
Step to the right:
Step together with left.

(Four counts)
8. SHUFFLE AND ROCK STEP *(Middle)*
Shuffle right, left, right:
Rock step back with left:
Step in place with right foot:
— the count is 'one & two, three, four' —

(Eight counts)
9. STEPS, TURNS AND STOMP *(Bottom*
Step to the side with the left foot:
Hold and clap:
Bring right foot to left foot:
— 'one, two &' —
Step to left:
Hold and clap:
Bring right foot to left foot:
Make a quarter turn as you step forward with left foot:
Step forward with right and make a half turn left:
Step in place with left foot:
Stomp right foot next to left.

TUSH PUSH

Music: T-R-O-U-B-L-E *by Travis Tritt.* Hollywood Nights *by Bob Seger*   **Choreographer:** *Jim Ferrazzano*
Walls: *Four*   **Counts:** *42*

(Four counts)
(*Top*) 1. **HEELS**
Right heel out and back.

(Four counts)
2. **HEELS**
Touch your right heel out and tap it twice.

(Two counts)
(*Middle*) 3. **JUMP AND HEELS**
Jump, touch your left heel out and back;

(Two counts)
4. **HEEL TAPS**
Touch your left heel out and tap it twice.

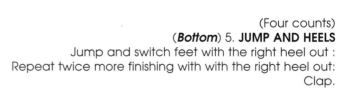

(Four counts)
(*Bottom*) 5. **JUMP AND HEELS**
Jump and switch feet with the right heel out :
Repeat twice more finishing with with the right heel out:
Clap.

(Four counts)
6. HIP BUMPS (*Top*)
Bump hips forward twice:
Bump hips backwards twice.

(Four counts)
7. GRIND
Swing hips forward and backwards, twice.

(Ten counts)
8. SHUFFLES AND ROCKS (*Middle*)
Shuffle forward, right, left, right:
Step forward on left foot:
Step back on right foot:
Shuffle backwards, left, right, left:
Step back on right foot:
Step forward on left foot:
Shuffle forward, right, left, right.

(Eight counts)
9. PIVOT AND SHUFFLES (*Bottom*)
Step forward on your left foot:
Half pivot turn to your right:
— you are facing the rear wall —
Shuffle forward, left, right, left:
Step forward on your right foot:
Half pivot turn to the left:
— you are facing the front again —
Step forward on your right foot and make a quarter turn to your left:
Stomp your right foot next to your left.

LIGHTENING CHA CHA

Music: We Dared the Lightning *by The Bellamy Brothers* **Choreographer:** *Gloria Johnson and Dusty Miller,*
Daytona, Florida **Walls:** *Four* **Counts:** *48*

(four counts)
(Top) s1. RIGHT TOE POINTS
Point right toe to right side and
Return;
Point right toe to right side and return;

(four counts)
(Middle) 2. RIGHT GRAPEVINE
WITH TURN Step right, cross left behind right, step right;
Make a quarter turn to the left;
(weight is on right foot);

(four counts)
3. LEFT TOE POINTS
Point left toe to left side and
Return;
Point left toe to left side and return;

(four counts)
(Bottom) 4. LEFT GRAPEVINE
Step left, cross left behind right;
Step left, tap right foot next to left;

(four counts)
5. CHA CHA AND ROCK — FORWARD
Right cha cha, right, left, right;
(the count is one & two);
Rock forward on left;
Rock backwards on right;

(four counts)
6. CHA CHA AND ROCK — BACKWARDS
Left cha cha, left, right, left;
(the count is one & two);
Rock backwards on right;
Rock forwards on left;

(two counts)
7. STEP AND TURN (*Top*)
Step forward on right;
Make a quarter turn to the left;

(six counts)
8. BACKWARD WEAVE (*Middle*)
Step right across left, step back on left;
Step back on right, step left across right;
Step back on right, step left next to right;

(four counts)
9. CHA CHA AND ROCK — FORWARD
Right cha cha, right, left, right;
(the count is one & two);
Rock forward on left;
Rock backwards on right

(four counts)
10. CHA CHA AND ROCK — BACKWARDS
Left cha cha, left, right, left;
(the count is one & two);
Rock backwards on right;
Rock forwards on left;

(two counts)
11. TURN AND CHA CHA (*Bottom*)
Cha cha, swing right over left and make a quarter turn
to the left at the same time;
(placing foot on floor to start the cha cha step: right,
left, right);

(six counts)
12. PIVOT TURN, CHA CHA, PIVOT TURN
Step forward on left;
Pivot half turn to right;
Left Cha cha left, right, left;
Step forward on right;
Pivot half turn left.

THE COWBOY

Music: I'm a Cowboy by The Smokin' Armadillos **Choreographer:** Unknown **Walls:** Two **Counts:** 48

(eight counts)
(Top) 1. **BACKWARD SHUFFLES**
Right shuffle back, right, left, right;
Left shuffle back, left, right, left;
Right shuffle back, right, left, right;
Left shuffle back, left, right, left;

(six counts)
(Middle) 2. **SHUFFLE FORWARD AND HALF PIVOT TURN**
Right shuffle forward, right, left, right;
Left shuffle forward, left, right, left;
Step forward on right;
Pivot half turn to the left;
(finish with weight on left);

(two counts)
3. **RIGHT KICK BALL CHANGE**
Kick right foot forward;
Step on ball of right and change weight to the left;

(eight counts)
4. **SHUFFLE BACKWARDS**
Right shuffle back, right, left, right;
Left shuffle back, left, right, left;
Right shuffle back, right, left, right;
Left shuffle back, left, right, left;

(six counts)
(Bottom) 5. **SHUFFLE FORWARD AND HALF TURN**
Right shuffle forward, right, left, right;
Left shuffle forward, left, right, left;
Step forward on right;
Pivot half turn to the left;
(finish with weight on left);

(two counts)
6. RIGHT KICK BALL CHANGE
Kick right foot forward;
Step on ball of right and change weight to the left;

(eight counts)
7. SIDE STEPS AND BUMPS *(Top)*
Step right, stomp left;
Bump hips right, left, right;
Step right, stomp left;
Bump hips right, left, right;

(eight counts)
8. SIDE STEP AND ROLLING RIGHT GRAPEVINE
Step right and touch left next to right;
Step left, cross right behind left;
Full turn stepping left, right, left, stomp right;

(four counts)
9. JUMPS AND HALF PIVOT TURN *(Middle and Bottom)*
Jump with feet slightly apart;
Jump and cross left in front of right;
Unwind by pivoting half turn to the right and clap;
(You will be facing rear wall);

(four counts)
10. TWO KICKS AND CHA CHA
Kick left foot forward twice;
Cha cha in place, left, right, left.

(Note: the count for the shuffle, cha cha and bumps is
'one & two')

THE CAST

WITH SPECIAL THANKS TO ANGELIQUE FERNANDEZ AND THE SUNSET STAMPEDE DANCERS WHO WERE: LEFT-TO-RIGHT

Harley Marshall
Hughie Thom
ANGELIQUE FERNANDEZ
Ian Lennie
Joanne White

Photography: TOBI CORNEY

Additional clothes supplies courtesy of R. SOLES at 109a Kings Road,
Chelsea, London SW3 4PA

If you would like further information about Sunset Stampede contact Angelique
Fernandez at PO Box 14503 London SW15 2ZT